VEGETARIAN
◇ CUISINE ◇

BY LOUISE GODWIN

EDITED BY MARION RAYMOND

BAY BOOKS SYDNEY & LONDON

Published by Bay Books
61-69 Anzac Parade, Kensington,
NSW 2033, Australia
©Bay Books
Photography by Howard Jones
National Library of Australia
Card number and ISBN 0 85835 389 X

Printed in Singapore
by Toppan Printing Company.
BBR887

Pottery used throughout this book was
supplied by Penelope Carr and John Edye
from Little Forest Pottery, Old
Hume Highway, Yerrinbool, near Mittagong,
New South Wales.

Contents

A word from the Editor   4

Vital vitamins   5

Crusty loaves and quick breads   7

Essential nutrition   16

Tasty nibbles   18

Unusual hot soups   27

Appetite stirrers   35

Recognise your pulses   45

Main events   46

Vegetable variations   59

Cool salads   69

For a sweet tooth   80

Weights and measures   91

Index   94

A word from the Editor

People choose to become vegetarians for many different reasons. They may be concerned about the ravages of man on his environment, about the slaughter of animals and the conditions under which this takes place, about the methods used to achieve rapid growth in animals, or they may simply prefer the taste of fruit and vegetables and enjoy the challenge of producing varied and imaginative meals without meat.

Most vegetarians believe that a meatless diet, or a diet free of all animal products, is beneficial. But, in order that the body obtain sufficient essential nutrients, a vegetarian diet has to be well-balanced and a thorough understanding of the nutritive value of foods is required. There are six classes of nutrients which are essential for our health and well-being: proteins, carbohydrates, fats, vitamins, minerals and water. Water exists in all foods to a greater or lesser extent so there is no need to provide a food group to represent it. Therefore, foods are grouped into five Basic Food Groups in such a way that each group represents a particular nutrient. (On page 17 you will find a chart which sets out the five Basic Food Groups, the nutrient each group represents and the recommended daily intake from each group.)

It is necessary to remember that no one food provides a sole nutrient; rather, certain groups of food provide more of one nutrient than any others. Many vegetarians seem to think that, providing they eat, say, quantities of soy beans, they will be getting all the protein the body requires. However, to be utilised fully protein needs the help of other nutrients.

Today vegetarians are divided into several categories: lacto-vegetarians, whose diets include dairy products; ovo-lacto-vegetarians, whose diets include eggs and dairy products; and vegans, who eat nothing but fruit, grains and vegetables. Only this last group is likely to suffer from dietary deficiencies. In the Zen macrobiotic diet the nutritional balance takes a back seat to the balance of *yin*, equated with acidity and expansion, and *yang*, connected with alkalinity and contraction, plus the need for love in cooking. This diet, with its ultimate goal of surviving exclusively on polished rice, is the most potentially dangerous.

The recipes in this book have been compiled by a nutritionist with the aim of producing attractive and appetising vegetarian meals which are, at the same time, well-balanced and nutritionally sound. It is often difficult to produce balanced meals containing enough variety and nutritive value without using dairy products and so some of the recipes include eggs, milk, butter, cheese, yoghurt and buttermilk.

For the true vegetarian, good meals are not necessarily built around traditional three course meals but, for convenience, the recipes in this book are collected into known categories. However, it is quite easy to use an entrée as a main course (and vice versa) simply by adjusting the quantities of the ingredients used. All the recipes are designed to serve between four and six people but one should bear in mind that a rice dish planned to serve this number as the only accompaniment to a meal may, in fact, serve far more when used in conjunction with other dishes.

As well as providing appetising family meals, many of the recipes are especially suitable for entertaining. They all produce interesting and varied dishes which even those who are not vegetarians will enjoy.

Vital vitamins

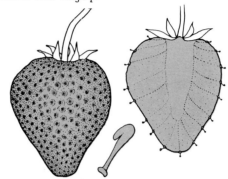

Of all nutritional elements, those that probably command the most attention are vitamins and minerals . . . and not the ones you get from a tablet. If your diet is well balanced, then the need for a vitamin supplement is unlikely to occur. A vegetarian diet certainly does not necessitate the use of supplements or expensive health foods in order to provide adequate amounts of vitamins because fresh fruit and vegetables are major sources of most vitamins.

Vitamins are often referred to as 'fat-soluble' or 'water-soluble'. The fat-soluble vitamins are A,D,E and K; the water-soluble vitamins are the B and C groups.

Vitamin A (retinol) is required for the growth and maintenance of the 'visual purple' in the eye and is also necessary for healthy cells in hair, skin and body membranes. It works closely with vitamin E. Vitamin A is found in yellow and green leafy vegetables and in fish oils, milk, butter and egg-yolk.

Vitamin D (calciferol) works with calcium and phosphorus and is important for strong bones and teeth. Vitamin D can be made by our bodies through the action of sunlight on the skin and it is found in foods such as cod-liver oil, sardines and salmon. Butter and milk provide smaller quantities.

Not all the functions of vitamin E (tocopherol) are known, although it has been used to treat such conditions as male infertility and habitual abortion. Vitamin E is found in wheat germ and the green leaves of spinach, lettuce and watercress.

Vitamin K (menadione) is a necessary factor in the blood-clotting mechanism. It is widely distributed in the green plant foods, with spinach, kale and cabbage being particularly good sources. Vitamin K is also synthesised by the action of bacteria in the intestinal tract.

Vitamin C (ascorbic acid) is essential for strong, healthy teeth, gums, bones and blood vessels. It is thought to increase resistance to infection and a lack of this vitamin delays the healing process. Fresh fruit and vegetables, especially oranges, lemons, tomatoes and rose hips, are excellent sources of vitamin C.

Many of the numerous vitamins in the B group are known by individual names such as thiamine, riboflavin, niacin, pantothenic acid, pyridoxin, cyanocobalamin and folic acid. Each member of the B group has a particular function but, generally speaking, they are the energy-releasing vitamins and are found in all living cells. Vitamin B and its compounds are provided by such foods as yeast, whole grain cereals, legumes and eggs.

The body uses many mineral elements. Some are referred to as trace elements because they are present in the body in extremely small amounts. The following minerals are listed in order of decreasing occurrence in the body: calcium, phosphorus, potassium, sulphur, sodium, chlorine, magnesium, copper, iodine, iron, and extremely small amounts of cobalt, selenium, zinc, fluorine and silicon.

Iron, the main function of which is the transfer of oxygen to various sites in the body, must command the greatest attention; a deficiency can result in nutritional anaemia. Liver is the best source and eggs contain useful amounts. Leafy green vegetables also contain appreciable amounts and there is some iron in pulses. Vegetarians should bear in mind that dehydration increases the concentration of certain nutrients, so that dried fruits, such as prunes, apricots and figs, are valuable sources of iron.

Iodine is an important element. It is used in the manufacture of thyroxine, a hormone produced in the thyroid gland, which controls metabolic rates. Sources of iodine are marine fish, iodised table salt (or sea salt) and vegetables grown in soils containing iodine.

Although calcium and phosphorus are not chemically similar, they occur together in the body, mainly in the bones. Calcium is dependent on vitamin D for its absorption from food. Milk in all its forms is an important source of calcium and no diet should be devoid of milk and cheese.

Phosphorus functions with calcium to give rigidity and it is also needed to form part of the enzyme systems involved in the metabolism of carbohydrates, fats and proteins. Vegetables alone can supply all the phosphorus the body requires although it is also found in animal products.

Sodium and potassium are essential minerals. Sodium is involved in maintaining water balance in cells, the pH of blood, and in conducting nervous impulses. Any food to which salt has been added is a source of sodium but it should be remembered that there is evidence that excessive intake of salt can cause hypertension. Potassium is present in the fluid within cells and is widely distributed in most commonly eaten foods.

Zinc is present in the body only in minute amounts but its presence is very important. It is a component of several enzymes and aids the transportation of carbon dioxide in the blood. It is also involved in the metabolism of protein into amino acids and in hormone production. Excellent sources of this mineral are oysters and other sea foods and whole grain cereals, legumes and pulses.

Crusty loaves and quick breads

Basic wholemeal bread

40g fresh yeast
1 teaspoon sugar
125ml milk
500g wholemeal flour
1 teaspoon salt
125ml warm water
1 tablespoon oil
extra milk

Heat milk to blood temperature, add sugar and crumbled yeast. (If the milk is too warm it will kill the yeast; if it is too cool the yeast will not be activated.) Set aside in a warm place until mixture is frothy. This should take about 10 minutes.

Place flour and salt in a bowl. Combine warm water and oil, stir into flour. The oil helps to keep the loaf fresh longer. Pour the frothy yeast mixture into the bowl and combine to form a smooth dough. If mixture is too stiff or too dry add some more warm milk. It is better to have the mixture slightly sticky at this stage because if it is too stiff the gas the yeast produces will not be able to escape and prove the dough. Yeast needs liquid in order to grow and develop.

Place dough in a warmed, lightly greased bowl and cover with a damp cloth. Put the bowl in a warm place and leave until dough has doubled in size. This is the process of proving and usually takes about 1 hour. If the dough does not appear to grow there are several possibilities: the dough may be either too cold or too hot, the yeast may be stale or it may have been killed earlier. If this occurs it is best to start again.

Pumpernickel, cottage oatmeal loaf and seed buns

Turn dough out onto a lightly floured board and knead well. Kneading is necessary to develop the gluten, a wheat protein which is very elastic if worked with moisture and warmth. To knead, punch the dough into a round flat shape, bring part of the edge back into the centre, then push down and out towards the edge again. Turn dough around. Take another part of the edge and repeat the kneading process. Continue this for at least 10 minutes until the dough becomes smooth and elastic. Test the dough by gently pressing with a dry finger; if it springs back, it is ready.

Shape dough into 2 loaves of equal size and place in oiled bread tins. Avoid creases and folds on the surface. Tins should be about two thirds full: if fuller, the dough may overflow; if less than half full, a very dense loaf may result. Cover tins with a damp cloth and set in a warm place until the dough has doubled in size or reaches the top of the tin. This should take about 30-45 minutes.

Bake loaves at 200°C for 20 minutes, reduce heat to 180°C and bake a further 30-40 minutes. To test, remove loaf from tin and tap gently on base. If it sounds hollow, the loaf is cooked. Place bread on a wire rack, cover with a dry, clean cloth and allow to cool. When freezing bread, be sure it is completely cold before wrapping and placing in freezer.

Pumpernickel

60g fresh yeast
½ cup lukewarm water
3 cups hot milk
½ cup molasses
1 tablespoon salt
2 tablespoons carraway seeds
3½ cups wholemeal flour
3½ cups rye flour

Dissolve yeast in warm water and set in a warm place until frothy. Mix hot milk with molasses and allow to cool. In a large bowl combine salt, carraway seeds and flours. Stir in yeast and milk mixtures. Combine to form a smooth dough, cover with a damp cloth and set in a warm place until dough has doubled in size. Turn out onto a floured board and knead thoroughly until dough is smooth and springy. Divide dough into 2 equal portions and roll into shape to fit bread tins. Cover with a damp cloth and set in a warm place until dough doubles in size. Bake at 200°C for 20 minutes, reduce to 180°C and bake a further 30-40 minutes or until loaves are cooked.

Anadama bread

150ml hot milk
150ml warm water
60g corn meal
1 tablespoon oil
3 tablespoons molasses
1 teaspoon salt
40g fresh yeast
375g wholemeal flour

Combine hot milk with half warm water and stir in corn meal. Add oil, molasses and salt. Crumble yeast into remaining warm water and allow to stand until frothy. Combine corn meal and yeast mixtures and beat in flour.

Place in floured bowl and beat until smooth and springy. Place dough in a greased bowl, cover with a damp cloth and leave to rise in a warm place until doubled in size. Turn out onto a board and knead until smooth and springy. Divide dough into 2 equal portions. Place in oiled bread tins, cover with a damp cloth and leave in a warm place to rise again until doubled in size. Bake at 190°C for 40-50 minutes.

Rye and soy loaf

40g fresh yeast
125ml warm milk
1 teaspoon sugar
300g wholemeal flour
100g rye flour
100g soy flour
1 teaspoon salt
125ml warm water
1 tablespoon oil
extra warm milk

Crumble yeast into warm milk with sugar. Stir to dissolve and set aside until frothy. Place flours and salt in large bowl. Combine warm water with oil and add to flour. Add frothy mixture. Combine to form a smooth dough, adding more milk if dough is too stiff. Cover with a damp cloth and set in a warm place until dough doubles in size. Turn out onto a board and knead thoroughly until dough is smooth and springy. Shape into 2 loaves of equal size. Place in oiled bread tins and press dents along centre of loaves with thumb. Cover with a damp cloth and set aside in a warm place until dough doubles in size. Bake at 200°C for 20 minutes, reduce to 180°C and bake a further 30-40 minutes.

Mixed grain loaf

30g fresh yeast
1½ cups warm milk
1 tablespoon sugar
1 tablespoon oil
3 cups wholemeal flour
1 cup plain flour
½ cup soy flour
1 cup bran
½ cup millet meal
1 tablespoon salt

Place yeast in bowl with ½ cup warm milk. Allow to stand until frothy. Add sugar, oil and remaining milk. Place remaining ingredients in a large bowl, stir in liquid and combine to a smooth dough. Cover with a damp cloth and set in a warm place until dough doubles in size. Turn out onto a board and knead until smooth and springy. Shape dough into 2 large round loaves and place on baking trays. Cover with a damp cloth and set in a warm place until dough again doubles in size. Bake at 200°C for 30-40 minutes.

Corn meal muffins

1 cup yellow corn meal
1 cup self-raising flour
1 teaspoon baking powder
1 cup milk
½ cup margarine
1 egg

If using cast iron muffin tins, pre-heat in oven while making mixture; other tins do not require heating. In a bowl, combine corn meal, flour and baking powder. Stir in milk. Melt margarine and stir into mixture with egg. Beat vigorously for 1 minute. Spoon mixture into tins, leaving them about three quarters full. Bake at 220°C for 10-12 minutes.

Gingerbread

½ cup butter
½ cup golden syrup
3 tablespoons brown sugar
2 tablespoons marmalade
½ cup milk
1 cup self-raising flour
1 cup wholemeal flour
2 teaspoons ground ginger
1 teaspoon mixed spice
½ teaspoon bicarbonate of soda
2 eggs
2 teaspoons grated glacè ginger

Place butter, syrup, sugar, marmalade and milk in a saucepan and heat gently until sugar dissolves and marmalade disperses. Allow to cool. Place dry ingredients in a bowl, pour in liquid mixture. Beat eggs lightly, stir into gingerbread. Mix well then spoon into greased, lined lamington tin. Sprinkle with grated ginger and bake at 180°C for 1 hour or until cooked.

Fruit and nut loaf, banana bran muffins and gingerbread

Seed buns

40g fresh yeast
¼ cup warm water
½ teaspoon sugar
¾ cup warm milk
½ cup buttermilk
1½ tablespoons honey
1½ cups plain flour
2½ cups wholemeal flour
1 teaspoon salt
½ tablespoon poppy seeds
½ tablespoon dill seeds
½ tablespoon carraway seeds
2 eggs
2 tablespoons water
sesame seeds for topping

Dissolve yeast in warm water and sugar. Set aside in a warm place until frothy. Add milk, buttermilk and honey. Combine flours, salt and poppy, dill and carraway seeds in a bowl and stir in liquid. Mix to a smooth dough. Cover with a damp cloth and leave in a warm place until dough doubles in size. Turn onto a lightly floured board and knead thoroughly until smooth and springy. Divide dough into 24 portions of equal size and shape into smooth, round buns. Place on greased oven slides, cover with a damp cloth and allow to stand in a warm place until doubled in size. Beat eggs with water and brush over buns. Sprinkle generously with sesame seeds and bake at 200°C for 20-25 minutes or until cooked.

Variations

Bowknots. Divide dough into pieces of even size and roll into sausage shapes 15cm long. Tie loosely in knots. Place on greased trays 2cm apart and allow to rise in a warm place until doubled in size. Bake as above.

Foldovers. Roll dough out to 1cm thickness. Cut out with 2-3cm pastry cutter and brush with melted butter. Fold each round in half and seal edges. Place rolls 2cm apart on greased baking sheet and allow to rise in a warm place until doubled in size. Bake as above.

Snips. Shape dough into round buns, cut a cross in top of each and allow to rise in a warm place until doubled in size. Bake as above.

Cottage oatmeal loaf

40g fresh yeast
15g sugar
475ml warm milk
170g plain flour
340g wholemeal flour
1 teaspoon salt
2 teaspoons oil
250g oats

Place yeast and sugar in a bowl with a little warm milk and allow to stand until frothy. Combine flours and salt in a large bowl. Stir yeast mixture and remaining milk into flour and combine to form a smooth dough. Cover with a damp cloth and set in a warm place until dough doubles in size.

Work in oats and oil until smooth. Turn out onto board and knead until uniform and springy. Divide dough into 2 equal portions and place into 18cm cake tins. Cover with a damp cloth and set aside in a warm place until the dough has doubled in size. Cut 4 slits in the top of each loaf. Bake at 200°C for 20 minutes, reduce to 180°C and bake a further 15-20 minutes or until loaves are cooked.

Cheese popovers

4 eggs
2 cups milk
2 cups wholemeal flour
¾ teaspoon baking powder
¼ teaspoon salt
½ teaspoon paprika
1 teaspoon chopped chives
½ cup grated cheese

Beat eggs with milk. Place flour in bowl with baking powder, salt, paprika and chives, stir in liquid. Beat thoroughly for 2 minutes. Spoon mixture into deep patty tins, leaving them one third full. Sprinkle with grated cheese and spoon in more mixture until tins are two thirds full. Bake at 220°C for 15 minutes, reduce to 190°C and bake a further 15-20 minutes, until popovers are brown and firm. Prick popovers with a skewer just before removing from oven. Serve warm.

Banana bran muffins

2 tablespoons margarine
¼ teaspoon vanilla essence
¼ cup sugar
1 cup wholemeal flour
1 cup bran
1 cup buttermilk
¾ teaspoon baking powder
1 ripe banana
1 egg
½ tablespoon honey

Melt margarine with sugar and vanilla essence. Allow to cool. Combine wholemeal flour, bran and baking powder in a bowl. Stir in buttermilk. Mash banana with egg and honey. Combine melted margarine and banana mixtures, add to flour and mix well. Spoon mixture into muffin tins, filling them two thirds full. Bake at 200°C for 20-25 minutes. Best eaten warm.

Fruit and nut twist

20g fresh yeast
¾ cup warm milk
2 tablespoons butter
¼ cup sugar
2 cups wholemeal flour
pinch salt
½ teaspoon mixed spice
½ cup mixed dried fruit
¼ cup chopped mixed nuts
1 egg

Dissolve yeast with a little sugar in ¼ cup warm milk and allow to stand in a warm place until frothy. Combine remaining milk with butter. Place flour, salt, mixed spice, fruit and nuts and remaining sugar in a bowl. Beat egg into milk and butter mixture. Pour all liquid into bowl and combine to form a smooth dough. Cover with a damp cloth and set in a warm place until dough doubles in size. Turn out onto floured board and knead thoroughly. Roll dough into a long sausage shape and then loop it into half. Take ends of dough and twist. Place on well-greased oven tray. Cover with a damp cloth and set in a warm place for 20 minutes.

Bake at 220°C for 15-20 minutes. As soon as twist is removed from oven, glaze with a lightly warmed mixture of 1 tablespoon water and 2 tablespoons sugar.

Essential nutrition

Before experimenting with a vegetarian diet one should first become fully acquainted with food values. It is important to remember that all nutrients are assisted in their function by a balance of other nutrients.

Protein provides the building blocks for the growth of cells and aids in the repair of damaged tissue. Proteins are composed of amino acids, the only substance to provide the body with nitrogen, which is vital for life.

There are twenty-two amino acids which are essential for good health. For adults, eight of these must be supplied daily in food because the body cannot make them. They are: lysine, leucine, isoleucine, valine, tryptophan, threonine, methionine and pheylananine. For children there is one additional essential amino acid, histidine, but the need for this is outgrown as the body develops and matures.

The other amino acids can be made in the body but, to ensure an adequate supply, they must also be present in our food. Often food containing the eight essential amino acids also contains some of the others. Food that supplies all of the eight amino acids in sufficient quantities is referred to as food of high biological value: meat, fish, poultry, eggs, milk and milk products.

As eggs and dairy products, such as milk, cheese and yoghurt, are foods of high biological value, the lacto or ovo-lacto-vegetarian need not be concerned with the possibility of a protein deficiency. Indeed, it is true to say that a diet which includes animal flesh, eggs and dairy products is really somewhat wasteful as there is almost an oversupply of protein of high biological value.

Complete vegans do not eat food that is in any way connected with an animal source. Their diet excludes meat, fish, poultry, eggs, dairy products and gelatine. Consequently, the protein source of a vegan is limited to nuts, legumes, grains, vegetables and fruit, which are all foods of low biological value. It is difficult for such a diet to provide adequate amounts of the essential amino acids.

Carbohydrate is a nutrient supplied by a large variety of foods and it has an important function. There are three types of carbohydrates: starches and sugars, which provide the body with energy, and cellulose, which is indigestible and provides the body with roughage. Nuts, legumes, starchy vegetables, grains and grain products are all sources of starch. Sweet fruit, vegetables, milk, honey and sugar provide the body with sugar. Whole grain cereals, vegetables and fruit are excellent sources of cellulose. Although fats provide a more concentrated source of energy for our bodies, carbohydrates are essential. Starches and sugars are more easily digested and metabolised by the body and so release energy more rapidly than fats.

Fats are needed for a number of reasons. They provide the body with essential fatty acids and fat soluble vitamins and they are the most concentrated source of energy. Fats also have a satiety value: they create a feeling of satisfaction and fullness.

Water is another essential nutrient. An adequate amount of water must be consumed daily if the body is to function efficiently. About two thirds of our body weight is water and, as it is constantly lost by body functions, it needs to be replaced. Water provides a means of transport for all the nutrients in the body and carries dissolved or suspended substances into cells. It also transports waste from the body and helps to maintain the correct body temperature. Water aids digestion as well as keeping mucous membranes moist in the mouth, nose, eyes and digestive system.

FOOD GROUP	NUTRIENT	RECOMMENED INTAKE
BREAD AND CEREALS	CARBOHYDRATES	3 serves per day (depends on energy requirements) 1 serve = 1 piece bread, ½ cup cereal
FRUITS AND VEGETABLES	VITAMINS AND MINERALS	At least 4 serves per day including 1 raw 1 serve = 1 piece fruit, ½ cup vegetable
MEAT, FISH, POULTRY, EGGS, NUTS, LEGUMES	PROTEIN	2-3 serves per day 1 serve = 90g
MILK AND MILK PRODUCTS	PROTEIN	Children – 600ml per day Adolescents – 600ml per day Adults – 300ml per day Pregnant and lactating women – 900ml per day 30g cheese = 200ml milk
FATS AND OILS	FAT	15-30g per day (depends on energy requirements and other food eaten)

Tasty nibbles

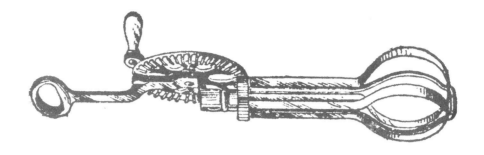

Rice croquettes with tomato dip

Rice croquettes

2 cups cooked brown rice
½ cup grated Swiss cheese
1 tablespoon chopped chives
1 tablespoon grated carrot
1 tablespoon self-raising flour
salt and pepper
2 eggs
oil for deep frying

Combine rice, cheese, chives and carrot. Mix in flour, salt and pepper. Separate eggs and beat yolks into rice mixture. Beat whites until stiff and fold into rice mixture. Heat oil for deep frying and drop teaspoons of mixture into hot oil. Deep fry until golden brown and serve warm with dip.

Dip

¼ cup mayonnaise
¼ cup yoghurt
¼ cup sour cream
1 tablespoon tomato purée
¼ teaspoon salt
¼ teaspoon cayenne pepper

Combine all ingredients until smooth and chill.

Vegetable pâté

1 leek
2 cups shelled peas
4 packed cups shredded spinach
1 egg
½ teaspoon tarragon
¼ teaspoon nutmeg
3 cups sliced carrots
½ teaspoon salt
¼ teaspoon pepper
¼ cup butter
½ cup water
2 tablespoons flour

Wash leek, slice white into thin rounds and steam until tender. Line a loaf tin with oiled greaseproof paper. Place cooked leek on paper. Cook peas in boiling water and steam spinach over them. When peas are just tender, drain well. Purée spinach and peas together with egg, tarragon and nutmeg. Spoon spinach layer into loaf tin and make level with spatula. Cook carrots with salt, pepper, butter and water until just tender. Drain off any remaining liquid and purée carrots with flour. Spoon carrot purée into tin and level with spatula. Rap tin on bench to remove any air bubbles.

Place greaseproof paper over pâté and cover with 3-4 layers of foil. Bake at 175°C for 1½ hours. Allow pâté to stand for 2 hours in refrigerator before turning out on serving platter. Delicious served with a fresh tomato sauce.

Hot cheese balls

3 tablespoons butter
½ teaspoon prepared mustard
salt and pepper
5 tablespoons plain flour
2 cups milk
180g Gruyère cheese
cornflour
2 eggs
dry breadcrumbs
oil for deep frying

Melt butter in saucepan with mustard, salt and pepper. Stir in flour until smooth. Gradually stir in milk until sauce thickens and boils. Pour sauce into a bowl, cover with plastic wrap and cool. Sprinkle baking tray with cornflour. Cut cheese into 1.5cm cubes. Coat cheese with sauce and place on tray. Place in refrigerator until set. Then roll balls in beaten egg, and coat with breadcrumbs. Chill in freezer while oil is heating. Deep fry balls until golden brown, drain and serve immediately.

Empanadas

1 onion
1 green capsicum
1 tablespoon olive oil
2 tomatoes
½ cup corn kernels
1 cup chopped mixed nuts
½ cup sliced peaches
2 tablespoons dry white wine
¼ teaspoon salt
2 cups soft breadcrumbs
1 pkt frozen puff pastry
1 cup melted butter

Peel and chop onion and capsicum finely. Heat oil and cook onion and capsicum for 5 minutes. Add peeled and chopped tomatoes and cook for 5 minutes. Add corn, nuts, peaches, wine and salt; stir gently while cooking. Add sufficient breadcrumbs to make a firm mixture, then allow to cool. Roll out pastry to 0.5cm thickness and cut out rounds of 10cm diameter. Brush edge of pastry with water, place teaspoons of mixture towards centre of each round. Fold pastry over to form half-moon shapes. Press edges together. Brush well with melted butter. Place empanadas on well greased baking sheet and bake at 200°C until golden brown.

Piquant apricots

250g fresh apricots
125g cream cheese
2 tablespoons mayonnaise
4 tablespoons chopped chives
1 tablespoon chopped parsley
salt and cayenne pepper
¼ red capsicum
lettuce, in cups or shredded

Cut apricots in half and remove stones. Set apricots aside in refrigerator. Beat cheese with mayonnaise until soft. Stir in chives, parsley, salt and pepper. Spoon mixture into halved apricots and place in refrigerator. Cut capsicum into thin shreds and prepare lettuce. Place lettuce on a platter, top with apricots and garnish with capsicum strips.

N.B. Well drained tinned apricots may be used when fresh are unavailable.

Piquant apricots

Cheese puffs

Pastry

90g butter
80ml milk
125g plain flour
60g Parmesan cheese
⅛ teaspoon pepper
3 eggs

Place butter and milk in saucepan and heat until butter melts. Stir to combine. Add flour, remove from heat. Add cheese and pepper. Beat mixture with a wooden spoon until mixture leaves sides of pan. Add 1 egg and beat thoroughly. Add another egg and beat until mixture is smooth. Add third egg and beat until mixture is shiny. Allow to cool. Drop teaspoons of mixture onto greased baking sheets and bake at 220°C for 25 minutes. Prick with toothpick to allow steam to escape. Remove from oven and cool puffs.

Filling

125g Roquefort cheese
1 Camembert
100g unsalted butter
2 tablespoons port
1 teaspoon chopped capers
chopped parsley for garnish

Crumble Roquefort into a bowl. Scoop centre out of Camembert. Combine cheeses with butter until mixture is smooth and creamy. Add port, capers, and blend well. Cut tops from puffs, scoop out dough from centre. Spoon cheese mixture into puffs, sprinkle with parsley and chill to serve.

Wholemeal salad tartlets

Pastry

125g plain flour
125g wholemeal flour
1 tablespoon chopped herbs
125g butter
1 egg yolk
2 tablespoons lemon juice
salt and pepper
iced water

Place flours and herbs in bowl and rub in butter. Add egg yolk, then lemon juice, salt, pepper and enough water to form dough. Wrap in plastic and allow to rest in refrigerator 20 minutes. Knead on a lightly floured board until smooth. Roll pastry to ½cm thickness and cut out with 8cm cutter. Place in patty tins and bake 10 minutes at 200°C. Cool.

Filling

½ cup asparagus cuts
¼ cup steamed peas
1 cup chopped tomatoes
¼ cup chopped celery
2 tablespoons chopped chives
¼ cup grated carrot
¼ cup corn kernels
yoghurt

Combine all vegetables and stir in enough yoghurt to hold filling together. Spoon into baked pastry shells and chill thoroughly before serving.

Wholemeal salad tartlets

Carrot and walnut tidbits

500g carrots
2 eggs
3 tablespoons wholemeal flour
salt and pepper
2 tablespoons parsley
¼ cup chopped onion
½ cup chopped walnuts
1 clove garlic
oil for frying
sesame seeds

Peel and chop carrots. Cook in small amount of water until tender. Drain. Process all ingredients, except oil and sesame seeds, in a blender until mixed to a paste. Chill. Form into small balls and roll in sesame seeds. Fry until golden in a little oil. Serve warm.

Spiced tomato appetisers

1 can tomatoes
¼ cup chopped onion
¼ cup grated carrot
½ cup corn meal
½ teaspoon salt
¼ teaspoon basil
¼ teaspoon cayenne pepper
1 tablespoon chopped peanuts

Chop and drain tomatoes to make 1¼ cups. Place tomatoes, onion and carrot in the top of a double boiler. Bring mixture to boil over direct heat. Stir in corn meal very slowly until well combined. Place top of double boiler over hot water and cook slowly for 1 hour until mixture is quite thick. Stir in finely chopped peanuts, salt, basil and pepper. Spoon mixture into greased 15cm square tin, smooth over and refrigerate until firm (overnight if possible). Cut into 2cm cubes and fry in a little oil until golden on all sides. Serve cubes on toothpicks with stuffed olives and a bowl of chilled yoghurt as a dip.

Potato sticks

250g potatoes
60g butter
2 egg yolks
125g self-raising flour
salt and pepper
1 tablespoon chopped chives
1 beaten egg
sesame seeds

Peel potatoes and cook in boiling salt water until tender. Drain and mash with egg yolks and butter until creamy. Beat in flour, salt, pepper and chives to form a dough. Chill. Roll out in a rectangle 1cm thick. Cut into sticks 1cm wide and 6cm long. Twist and brush lightly with beaten egg. Place on a greased oven tray, sprinkle with sesame seeds and bake at 200°C for 10 minutes or until golden brown and crisp. Leave on oven tray until cool.

Potato sticks

Vegetable pâté

☛ *Unusual hot soups*

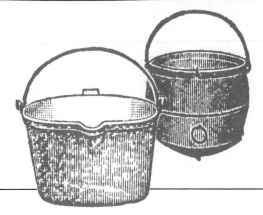

Basic light vegetable stock

2 large onions
4 sticks celery
4 medium carrots
2 medium parsnips
½ cup chopped parsley
2 teaspoons white peppercorns
3 teaspoons rock salt
3 bay leaves
3 litres water

Peel and chop onions roughly. Wash and chop celery, carrots and parsnips. Place all vegetables in a large saucepan and add salt, pepper and bay leaves. Pour in water, cover saucepan and simmer for at least 2 hours. Strain stock before use.

Basic dark vegetable stock

2 large onions
2 tablespoons butter
4 sticks celery
4 medium carrots
2 medium parsnips
½ cup chopped parsley
2 teaspoons black peppercorns
3 teaspoons rock salt
3 bay leaves
3 litres water

Peel and chop onions roughly. Melt butter in large saucepan and fry onion until very brown. While onion is cooking wash and roughly chop celery, carrots, and parsnips. Add to onions and stir well. Add all remaining ingredients to saucepan, cover and simmer for at least 2 hours. Strain stock before use.

Almond and grape soup

1 cup blanched almonds
1 cup milk
1 onion
1 stick celery
1 tablespoon oil
5 cups basic dark stock (recipe this page)
2 cups black grapes
2 egg yolks
3 tablespoons cream
1 tablespoon chopped parsley

Place almonds and milk in saucepan and bring to boil. Remove from heat and allow to stand 1 hour. Peel and chop onion and celery, cook in oil until soft. Place celery and onion in saucepan with stock and 1½ cups peeled and pitted grapes. Simmer 15 minutes and purée. Set aside. Purée almonds and milk in blender. Add almond mixture to soup and reheat in saucepan. Blend egg yolks and cream, add a little warm soup then stir into soup. Do not boil. Serve soup garnished with reserved ½ cup grapes and parsley.

Almond and grape soup

Cream of watercress soup

1 bunch watercress
1 tablespoon butter
2 tablespoons chopped onion
1 tablespoon plain flour
3 cups hot milk
1 cup basic light stock (recipe p. 28)
salt and pepper to taste
1 egg
8 tablespoons cream
watercress or avocado to garnish

Trim watercress and remove stalks. Sweat watercress and onion gently with butter. When wilted, blend in flour, then hot milk and stock. Stir until mixture thickens and boils. Add a little salt and pepper and simmer soup 10 minutes. Blend soup and return to pan. Mix egg with cream, add a little hot soup then add mixture to simmering soup. Do not allow to boil. Serve garnished with small sprig of watercress or a slice of fresh avocado.

Buttermilk soup

1 small cucumber
salt
3 cups basic light stock (recipe p. 28)
3 cups buttermilk
1 teaspoon prepared French mustard
2 tablespoons minced celery
2 teaspoons chopped chives
2 teaspoons chopped fresh dill
2 teaspoons chopped parsley

Peel and dice cucumber very finely. Sprinkle with salt and allow to stand 30 minutes. Rinse in cold water to remove excess salt. Mix all ingredients in large bowl and chill thoroughly.

Cream of choko soup

6 chokos
1 onion
1 stick celery
½ cup rice
6 cups basic light stock (recipe p. 28)
salt and pepper
1 clove garlic, crushed
½ cup sour cream

Peel chokos, remove hard centre and chop. Peel and chop onion and celery. Place chokos, onion, celery, rice, stock, salt, pepper and garlic in saucepan and simmer for 45 minutes. Purée soup in blender or through a sieve. Return to heat and stir in sour cream. Do not boil. May be served with additional sour cream.

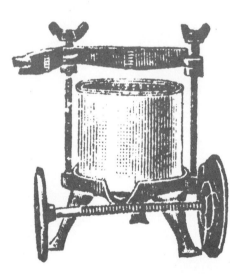

Cream of watercress soup

Two bean soup

¼ cup yellow split peas
¼ cup red kidney beans
¼ cup lima beans
¼ cup chick peas
6 cups basic light stock (recipe p. 28)
salt and pepper
½ cup chopped onions
½ cup chopped red capsicum
¼ cup chopped celery
¼ cup chopped carrots
1 tablespoon chopped parsley
1 chopped clove garlic
2 tablespoons oil
4 cups basic dark stock (recipe p. 28)
1 bay leaf
⅛ teaspoon marjoram
⅛ teaspoon basil
½ cup chopped, peeled tomatoes

Soak beans and peas overnight in light stock with salt and pepper. Cook until tender. Discard liquid. Place onion, capsicum, celery, carrot, parsley and garlic in large saucepan with oil and cook 5 minutes. Pour in dark stock and simmer until vegetables are tender. Add beans and peas and all remaining ingredients, simmer 20 minutes. Remove bay leaf before serving.

Plum soup

1kg purple plums
8 cups basic dark stock (recipe p. 28)
¼ cup lemon juice
2 cardamom pods
½ cup sugar
3 tablespoons cornflour
3 tablespoons brandy
1 cup sour cream

Cut plums in half and remove stones. Place in a large saucepan with stock and simmer gently for 2 minutes. Remove all skins from plums and purée in a blender or through a sieve. Place purée in saucepan with lemon juice, cardamom pods and sugar. Bring soup to the boil and simmer until sugar dissolves. Remove cardamom pods and discard. Remove one cup of soup from saucepan and cool it. Blend cornflour with brandy, stir into cup of cooled soup and add mixture to soup in saucepan. Stir until soup thickens and boils. Simmer 3 minutes. Chill soup. To serve, pour soup over a bowl of crushed ice and swirl in sour cream.

Plum soup

Pea and barley soup

½ cup barley
2 cups water
4 cups basic dark stock (recipe p. 28)
1 tablespoon butter
1 tablespoon flour
salt and pepper
½ cup milk
1 carrot
1 cup green peas
1 tablespoon chopped chives for garnish.

Soak barley in water overnight. Drain, rinse and add to saucepan with stock. Cover and simmer about 1 hour until barley is tender. Strain, reserving 4 tablespoons of cooked barley. Melt butter and stir in flour, salt, pepper and cook 1 minute. Add to strained stock and stir over medium heat until mixture thickens and boils. Add milk and reserved barley. Allow to simmer while preparing vegetables. Peel carrot and cut into long thin strips. Cook with peas in water until just tender. Drain, add to soup and serve garnished with chives.

Farmhouse chowder

1½ cups diced potato
½ cup chopped onion
¼ cup chopped celery
2 tablespoons chopped parsley
½ cup grated carrot
4 cups basic dark stock (recipe p. 28)
salt and pepper
1 cup cream
1 cup grated cheese
¼ teaspoon dry mustard
1 teaspoon soy sauce
1 teaspoon basil
extra stock
2 tablespoons chopped chives for garnish

Place potato, onion, celery, parsley and carrot in saucepan with stock, salt and pepper. Simmer until potato is tender. Heat cream and stir in cheese until melted. Add to soup with mustard, soy sauce and basil. Stir gently; do not allow to boil. If soup is too thick add more stock. Serve sprinkled with chives.

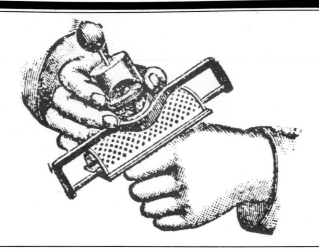

Asparagus timbales

1kg asparagus
2 eggs
1 egg yolk
salt and pepper
⅛ teaspoon nutmeg
2 tablespoons chopped parsley
4 thin strips red capsicum
4 lettuce leaves

Steam asparagus until tender. Remove 12 tips and reserve for garnish. Purée remaining asparagus in blender and sieve purée if any coarse fibres remain. Place mixture in saucepan and simmer to reduce by one third, stirring frequently. Remove from heat. Combine eggs, egg yolk, salt, pepper and nutmeg. Whisk into asparagus purée. Grease 4 small ovenproof dishes and sprinkle with finely chopped parsley. Pour mixture into prepared dishes and place in baking dish half filled with cold water.

Bake at 190°C for 1 hour. After half an hour cover pots with foil. When cooked, remove dishes from water and allow to stand 5 minutes. Place a lettuce leaf on each serving plate and turn out onto lettuce. Decorate each serving with 3 asparagus tips and 1 strip of capsicum. Serve immediately.

Stuffed turnips

4 small turnips
2 tablespoons butter
sprig fresh rosemary
1 cup mashed potato
2 tablespoons grated onion
salt and pepper
2 teaspoons chopped parsley
juice 1 lemon

Wash turnips, peel but do not cut off base. Cook turnips in boiling salted water until tender but still firm. Cut a lid off each one, scoop out centre, leaving the outer part as a cup. Reserve pulp. Stand turnip cups in melted butter and fry for 1 minute with crumbled rosemary. Mash turnip pulp and potato until creamy. Beat in salt, pepper and onion. Spoon filling back into turnip cups. Place in baking dish and sprinkle with parsley and lemon juice. Bake at 200°C for 10 minutes.

Stuffed turnips

Spinach rolls

4 dried Chinese mushrooms
1 shallot
1 clove garlic
2 tablespoons oil
1 teaspoon ginger
1 cup shredded cabbage
½ cup chopped celery
½ cup grated carrot
1 cup fresh bean sprouts
¼ cup chopped water chestnuts
2 tablespoons soy sauce
1 tablespoon sesame oil
1 tablespoon dry sherry
2 tablespoons cornflour
salt and pepper
1 bunch spinach

Soak mushrooms in warm water 10 minutes. Remove stalks, drain and slice. Chop shallot and crush garlic. Heat oil, stir fry mushrooms, shallot and garlic 3 minutes. Add ginger, cabbage, celery, carrot, bean sprouts and water chestnuts. Cook 5 minutes. Combine soy sauce, sesame oil and sherry; blend in cornflour and stir into vegetables. Adjust seasoning and cook mixture until it thickens and boils. Cool. Wash spinach and remove hard stems. If large, cut spinach leaves into shapes about 12cm square. If small, use whole spinach leaves. Place a tablespoon of mixture on each spinach leaf, roll up and seal ends. Steam rolls over boiling water until spinach is tender. Serve hot.

Crunchy nut terrine

1½ cups chopped celery
1½ cups chopped onion
2 tablespoons oil
½ cup almond meal
1 cup chopped walnuts
1 cup toasted, chopped cashew nuts
¼ cup rolled oats
1 tablespoon sesame seeds
250g cottage cheese
3 eggs
1 teaspoon salt
¼ teaspoon black pepper
1 teaspoon chopped parsley
¼ teaspoon marjoram

Heat oil and cook celery and onion until golden. Combine with all remaining ingredients and mix thoroughly. Grease and line 2 bar tins and spoon half mixture into each. Bake at 180°C for 45 minutes and test for firmness. If not firm continue to bake a little longer. Turn out onto plate, remove paper and cool slightly. Serve terrine surrounded with lettuce cups filled with tomato slices and celery sticks. A good party dish which goes a long way.

Crunchy nut terrine

Mushroom casserole

500g mushrooms
1 onion
2 tomatoes
2 tablespoons butter
2 cups cooked long grain rice
½ cup sour cream
1 egg
1 tablespoon chopped parsley
salt and pepper
¼ teaspoon nutmeg

Wash and slice mushrooms. Peel and slice onion, peel and chop tomatoes. Melt butter in saucepan and cook onions 5 minutes. Add mushrooms and tomatoes. Cook further 5 minutes. Spoon mixture into 4 ramekins. Combine rice, sour cream, egg, parsley, salt, pepper and nutmeg. Spread over mushroom mixture in ramekins and bake at 180°C for 20 minutes. Leave to stand 10 minutes before serving.

Tomato granita

8 tomatoes
2 shallots
1 stick celery
1 clove garlic
1 cucumber
1 teaspoon chopped mint

Peel tomatoes and chop finely. Strain to remove excess liquid and remove seeds. Chop shallots and celery finely, and crush garlic. Combine tomatoes, shallots, celery and garlic. Pour mixture into freezer trays and freeze. Remove from freezer 10 minutes before serving to soften ice a little. Peel cucumber and chop into very small dice. Break up tomato ice with a fork and stir in cucumber and mint. Serve in individual glass dishes.

Vegetable tacos

1 pkt taco shells
oil for frying

Filling

2 tablespoons butter
2 tablespoons flour
salt and pepper
1½ cups milk
2 hard-boiled eggs
½ cup sliced mushrooms
½ cup grated carrot
2 tablespoons chopped shallots
1 cup finely shredded spinach
½ cup grated cheese

Melt butter in saucepan, add flour and seasoning, stir until smooth. Stir milk in gradually to make a smooth sauce, cook until thickened. Peel and chop eggs. To hot sauce add egg, mushrooms, carrot, shallots and spinach. Combine and cook 10 minutes. Meanwhile cook taco shells in fry pan with a little oil until golden brown on both sides. Stir cheese into filling and cook one minute. Spoon mixture into taco shells and stand upright in ovenproof serving dish. Sprinkle with chopped parsley and paprika. Reheat in oven to serve.

Tomato granita

Mushroom custards

12 medium-sized mushrooms
125g fetta cheese
½ teaspoon chopped dill
4 eggs
500ml milk
salt and pepper

Wash mushrooms and remove stalks. Combine fetta cheese with dill and fill mushroom caps with cheese. Place them, cheese side up, in 4 individual gratin dishes. Lightly beat eggs, stir in milk, salt and pepper. Pour an equal amount of mixture into each dish. Stand dishes in baking dish containing enough cold water to reach half way up dishes. Bake at 180°C until custard sets (45-60 minutes).

Vegeroni Alfredo

250g Vegeroni noodles
2 shallots
¾ cup cream
½ cup Parmesan cheese
1 cup champignon mushrooms
1 cup canned corn kernels, drained
salt and pepper
¼ teaspoon nutmeg

Cook noodles in boiling salt water until tender. Drain, rinse, and keep warm in colander over simmering water. Wash and chop shallots and combine with cream and Parmesan cheese. Heat mixture through gently but do not boil. Stir in mushrooms, corn, salt, pepper and nutmeg. Place noodles in 4 ramekins. Pour sauce over and stir to combine. Heat through in moderate oven before serving.

Pears in tarragon

3 soft pears
2 cups water
1 egg
1 tablespoon castor sugar
3 tablespoons tarragon vinegar
salt and pepper
½ cup cream
6 lettuce cups
2 teaspoons chopped tarragon
paprika

Peel pears, cut in halves lengthwise and remove core. Place flat side down in a baking dish and pour in water. Cover with foil and bake at 185°C for 20 minutes or until just tender. Drain and cool. Break egg into a bowl, beat lightly with a fork, add sugar, gradually add vinegar. Add salt and pepper. Place bowl over saucepan of hot water and stir with wooden spoon until sauce begins to thicken. Remove saucepan from heat and continue to stir as sauce thickens. Remove bowl from saucepan and continue to stir a few minutes more. Cover and cool. Beat cream until slightly fluffy then fold into cooled sauce with chopped tarragon. Place pears in individual lettuce cups, flat side down and coat with sauce. Dust with paprika and serve.

Pears in tarragon

Black-eyed Susans

185g black-eyed beans
1 onion
1 tomato
½ cup tomato purèe
2 eggs
¼ teaspoon salt and pepper

Cover beans with warm water and leave to stand overnight. Drain and remove skins. Peel and chop onion and tomato. Place beans, onion, tomato and tomato purée in a blender and process. Add eggs, salt, pepper, and blend until smooth. Pour into 4 ramekins and place in a baking dish containing a little cold water. Bake at 180°C for 30 minutes or until firm.

Roquefort mousse

125g Roquefort cheese
125g cottage cheese
1 tablespoon chopped chives
1 tablespoon gelatine
4 tablespoons cold water
½ cup cream
4 egg whites
4-6 lettuce cups

Beat cheeses and chives together until smooth. Combine gelatine with water in a bowl and stand over hot water. Stir until dissolved. Combine with cream and stir into cheese mixture. Beat egg whites until stiff and fold into cheese mixture. Spoon mousse into 4 to 6 individual moulds and chill until set. Turn out of moulds into lettuce cups to serve.

N.B. Blue vein or Blue Castello cheese may be used instead.

Soyaroni casserole

250g Soyaroni noodles
2 tablespoons butter
2 tablespoons flour
1 teaspoon prepared mustard
3 cups milk
1½ cups grated Edam cheese
salt and pepper
1 teaspoon chopped dill
2 tablespoons chopped gherkin
1 cup soft breadcrumbs

Cook noodles in boiling salt water until tender. Drain, rinse and keep warm in colander over simmering water. Melt butter in a saucepan, stir in flour and mustard. Gradually add milk, stirring constantly until sauce thickens and boils. Reduce heat, cook 3 minutes. Stir in 1 cup of grated cheese. Allow cheese to melt into sauce, then add salt, pepper, dill and gherkin. Combine sauce with noodles and place in 4 individual ramekins. Combine breadcrumbs with remaining cheese and sprinkle over top. Bake at 180°C for 15 minutes, place under griller to brown before serving.

Recognise your pulses

Dried peas, beans and lentils are the edible seeds of vegetables known collectively as pulses or legumes. All pulses are rich in protein of low biological value, with the exception of soy beans: here the protein content is almost the equivalent of meat.

Most pulses can be sprouted successfully; the sprouts have the added value of vitamin C as well as containing protein and valuable minerals.

Pulses can be used in a variety of dishes, are easy to prepare, and need very little supervision while cooking. They add colour, texture and flavour and are good extenders to make a filling meal.

Lima beans are pale green or creamy coloured and can be served in soups, casseroles, mixed with corn or used in salads.

Split peas can be orange, yellow or green and are generally used in soups.

Mung beans are small, green, and widely used for growing the familiar bean sprout.

Kidney beans are shiny, deep red, and kidney shaped; excellent used in soups or casseroles.

Borlotti beans are a pretty, speckled, reddish brown and are perfect for soups and casseroles.

Haricot beans are smooth, creamy, slightly flat beans and come in many sizes; they have many uses.

Chick peas, also known as garbanzo beans, are creamy coloured nut-like peas popular for soups, stews, and even served cold in salads. Used in dishes such as hummus and felafel, chick peas can also be sprouted.

Lentils come in various colours and sizes and can be bought whole or split. They are often added to soups and stews as a thickening agent and can also be used for patties, baked vegetable loaves, and make very good purée.

Soy beans are the most nutritious beans of all and can be sprouted with great success. They are very versatile and, when manufactured, come in many guises.

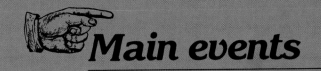

Individual moussakas

4 small eggplants
1 tablespoon butter
1 tablespoon flour
½ teaspoon nutmeg
salt and pepper
¾ cup milk
¼ cup cream
2 onions
2 cloves garlic
1 tablespoon oil
2 tomatoes
2 cups cooked soy beans
1 tablespoon chopped parsley
¼ teaspoon oregano
1 cup grated Cheddar cheese
½ cup soft breadcrumbs

Slice eggplant in half lengthwise, scoop out seeds, leaving flesh. Sprinkle with salt, turn upside down and allow to stand 30 minutes. Melt butter in saucepan, stir in flour, nutmeg, salt and pepper; cook one minute. Gradually add milk, stirring until sauce thickens and boils. Cool slightly, stir in cream, cover and set aside. Peel and chop onions and garlic, cook in oil 5 minutes. Add peeled, chopped tomatoes, soy beans, parsley and oregano. Simmer 15 minutes. Rinse eggplant, pat dry, place in baking dish. Spoon equal quantities of mixture into each half. Cover with white sauce. Combine grated cheese and breadcrumbs, and sprinkle on top. Bake at 180°C until eggplant is soft but not split. Place under griller to brown top before serving.

Okra casserole

1 eggplant
2 carrots
2 potatoes
2 onions
¼ cup olive oil
4 zucchini
4 tomatoes
2 cups okra, canned or fresh
¼ cup chopped parsley
2 teaspoons oregano
salt and pepper
¼ teaspoon nutmeg

Slice eggplant, sprinkle with salt and leave to stand 30 minutes. Peel carrots, potatoes and slice; place in boiling water and simmer 5 minutes. Drain and rinse under cold water. Peel and slice onions. Rinse eggplant and pat dry. Heat oil, fry onions until soft. Remove and fry eggplant until golden. Slice zucchini and tomatoes. Top and tail okra. In a deep casserole layer all vegetables, sprinkling each layer with a little parsley, oregano, salt and pepper and nutmeg. Cover casserole and bake at 190°C 1 hour or until tender.

Individual moussakas

Okra casserole

Spinach roulade

Filling

350g mushrooms
1 tablespoon butter
1 tablespoon flour
salt and pepper
¾ cup milk
6 tablespoons cream
½ teaspoon nutmeg
tomato slices

Wash mushrooms and slice finely. Cook in butter 10 minutes. Add flour, salt, pepper, and stir well. Combine milk, cream and nutmeg. Add to mushrooms and stir until mixture thickens and boils. Simmer 2 minutes and keep warm while preparing roulade.

Roulade

½kg spinach
1 tablespoon butter
salt and pepper
4 egg yolks
4 egg whites
Parmesan cheese

Wash spinach, remove stems and chop finely. Heat butter in saucepan with salt and pepper and cook spinach until wilted. Drain and purée in blender. Stir in egg yolks. Beat egg whites until stiff and fold gently into spinach mixture. Spoon into a greased and lined Swiss roll tin. Spread evenly and sprinkle with a little Parmesan cheese. Bake at 200°C for 10-15 minutes, until roulade is firm to the touch and well risen. Turn out onto damp tea towel and peel off paper. Spread with mushroom filling, roll up. Place on warm serving plate and decorate with tomato slices to serve.

Cuban eggs

2 onions
2 green apples
2 carrots
2 tablespoons oil
½ cup plain flour
⅛ teaspoon salt
2 teaspoons curry powder
3 cups vegetable stock
3 cups cooked brown rice
juice 2 lemons
12 hard-boiled eggs, halved
1 banana
½ cup sultanas
½ cup roasted cashews

Peel and dice onions, apples and carrots. Fry in hot oil for 5 minutes. Stir in flour, salt and curry powder. Gradually stir in stock until smooth. Stir until sauce thickens and boils. Keep hot. Place brown rice in shallow casserole and pour over lemon juice. Place eggs on rice, cut side down. Peel and cut banana into 2cm pieces. Place banana, sultanas and cashews on eggs. Pour hot sauce over. Cover casserole and cook for 15 minutes at 180°C.

Spinach roulade

Baked vegetable ring

2 onions
2 cloves garlic
1 tablespoon oil
1 bunch spinach
2 cups cottage cheese
2 cups cooked soy beans
½ cup chopped walnuts
½ cup sultanas
¼ cup tomato paste
¼ cup grated carrot
¼ teaspoon dill
salt and pepper
tomato, sliced

Peel and chop onions and garlic, fry in oil until soft but not brown. Wash spinach and remove stalks. Steam until just tender. Chop finely and drain in a colander. Squeeze spinach to remove all excess liquid. Combine spinach with cooked onion and all remaining ingredients. Grease and line a ring tin. Place slices of tomato on base of dish. Cover with spinach mixture and press down firmly. Cover tin with foil and bake at 180°C for 45 minutes, removing foil after 25 minutes. If not firm after 45 minutes bake 10 minutes more. Allow to stand 10 minutes before turning out onto serving plate. Fill centre with fresh tomato filling and serve.

Fresh tomato filling

2 tomatoes
¼ cup chopped onion
1 tablespoon chopped mint
1 tablespoon lemon juice
⅛ teaspoon cayenne
⅛ teaspoon salt

Peel and chop tomatoes. Combine with all remaining ingredients and fill centre of vegetable ring.

Ribbon bean bake

1 onion, chopped
1 clove garlic, finely chopped
1 tablespoon olive oil
¼ cup chopped celery
1 tablespoon chilli sauce
½ cup tomato purée
¼ cup tomato paste
¼ cup red wine
½ teaspoon salt
¼ teaspoon pepper
¼ teaspoon oregano
¼ teaspoon basil
½ cup cooked butter beans
½ cup cooked chick peas
½ cup cooked red kidney beans
1 cup cooked soy beans
½ cup cooked lima beans
250g Mozzarella cheese
250g Ricotta cheese
Parmesan cheese

Heat oil and cook onion, garlic and celery 5 minutes. Add chilli sauce, tomato purée and paste, wine, salt, pepper, oregano and basil. Simmer 25 minutes. Combine all beans and peas in a bowl. Slice Mozzarella cheese thinly. Beat Ricotta cheese in a bowl until smooth. Place one third tomato sauce in bottom of medium-sized casserole. Spoon in one third bean mixture and spread one third Ricotta cheese over beans. Place one third Mozzarella cheese on Ricotta. Repeat layers twice and sprinkle finished casserole with Parmesan cheese. Cover and bake for 30 minutes at 190°C. Remove cover and bake 10 minutes more to brown.

Baked vegetable ring

Bean-filled marrow

1 marrow

Stuffing

1 onion
1 clove garlic
1 cup soaked soy beans
½ cup soaked red kidney beans
½ cup soft breadcrumbs
3 tablespoons tomato paste
1 cup grated Cheddar cheese
¼ teaspoon salt
¼ teaspoon cayenne

Prepare stuffing: peel and chop onion, place onion and all remaining ingredients in a blender and make a smooth mixture, do not purée. Cut marrow in half lengthwise and scoop out seeds. Fill cavities with stuffing and place in baking dish. Pour water to a level of 2cm in dish. Cover with foil and bake at 190°C until marrow is tender.
N.B. Filling is also suitable for capsicums, zucchini or butternut pumpkin.

Rice pie

1½ cups cooked rice
1 tablespoon butter
2 eggs
1 cup grated cheese
½ cup chopped onion
1 cup chopped celery
1 tablespoon oil
1 cup sliced zucchini
1 cup sliced mushroom
½ cup cream
2 eggs
salt and pepper
1 teaspoon chopped mint
1 sliced tomato

Add butter and lightly beaten eggs to rice while still hot. Press into 23cm pie plate and sprinkle with half of the grated cheese. Fry onion and celery in oil until tender; place in pie, sprinkle remaining cheese over. Layer zucchini and mushrooms into pie. Combine cream, eggs, salt, pepper, mint, and pour into pie. Bake at 190°C for 35 minutes or until pie is set. During last 5 minutes of cooking place slices of tomato on top for garnish.

Rice pie

Instant bean medley

1 onion, chopped
1 red capsicum, chopped
1 tablespoon oil
1 can soy beans
1 can red kidney beans
1 can lima beans
1 can butter beans
1 can champignon mushrooms
1 can corn kernels
1 can asparagus cuts
1 can whole tomatoes
salt and pepper
½ teaspoon chilli powder
1 tablespoon chopped chives
1 cup grated Cheddar cheese
½ cup soft breadcrumbs

Heat oil and drain all cans. Place all ingredients, except cheese and breadcrumbs, in a greased casserole. Combine cheese and breadcrumbs, sprinkle on top. Bake for 20 minutes at 190°C. Place under griller to brown top before serving.

Hot rice salad

1 cup cooked brown rice
1 onion
1 stick celery
2 tablespoons butter
¼ cup chopped red capsicum
1 cup sliced mushrooms
2 spinach leaves
2 hard boiled eggs
salt and pepper
¼ teaspoon paprika
½ cup sour cream
¼ cup slivered almonds

Keep cooked rice hot in colander over hot water. Peel and chop onion and celery. Melt butter in fry pan and cook onion, celery, capsicum and mushrooms for 5 minutes. Add to hot rice. Wash and chop spinach finely and add to hot rice. Peel and chop eggs and place in saucepan with salt, pepper, paprika and sour cream. Heat but do not boil. Place salad in serving bowl. Pour sour cream dressing over salad. Sprinkle with almonds to serve.

Flan indienne

Pastry

¼ cup plain flour
¾ cup plain wholemeal flour
salt
6 tablespoons butter
1 egg
iced water
egg white

Mix both flours in bowl with salt. Rub in butter and egg. Add enough iced water to make a firm dough. Wrap in plastic and refrigerate 20 minutes. Roll out to line 20cm flan tin. Refrigerate 10 minutes. Cover pastry with a piece of greaseproof paper and sprinkle with noodles or rice. Bake blind at 190°C for 15 minutes. Remove paper and filling, brush pastry with egg white to seal.

Filling

½ cup chopped onion
½ cup chopped celery
1 tablespoon oil
2 teaspoons curry powder
1 tablespoon butter
1 tablespoon flour
¾ cup milk
2 hard boiled eggs
½ cup cooked brown rice
½ cup sliced mushrooms

Fry onion and celery in oil. Add curry, butter and flour. Stir in milk until sauce thickens and boils. Peel and slice eggs and place in flan. Add rice, then mushrooms and pour over sauce. Bake at 180°C for 20 minutes. Allow to stand 5 minutes before slicing.

Crispy cheese flan

Crust

125g crisp cheese-flavoured biscuits
3 tablespoons butter
¼ cup grated Gruyère cheese
salt and pepper
1 teaspoon prepared French mustard
extra butter

Crush biscuits finely and place in bowl. Stir in melted butter, grated cheese, salt, pepper and mustard. Grease a 20cm flan dish and press crumb mixture over base and up sides of dish. Press in firmly with back of spoon. Bake at 180°C for 10 minutes, then allow to cool.

Filling

1 onion, chopped
1 clove garlic, crushed
1 tablespoon oil
4 tomatoes, peeled and chopped
salt and pepper
½ teaspoon basil
2 whole canned pimentoes
6 eggs
3 tablespoons cream
fresh chopped mixed herbs

Heat oil in large pan and cook onion and garlic until soft. Add tomatoes to pan with salt, pepper, basil and chopped pimento. Bring to boil and simmer until mixture is thick and pulpy. Beat eggs and cream together, stir into tomato mixture until mixture thickens. Allow to cool slightly then spoon into shell. Sprinkle with freshly chopped herbs and chill before serving.

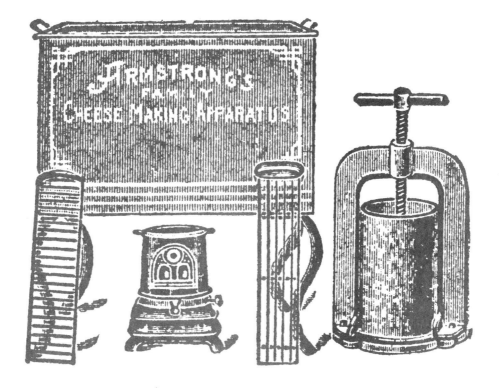

Crunchy onion pie

150g carrots
1kg onions
250g mushrooms
6 green cabbage leaves
2 eggs
1 tablespoon milk powder
½ cup water
¼ teaspoon thyme
40g pine nuts
40g hazelnuts
40g cashews
40g margarine
100g soft brown breadcrumbs
1 teaspoon yeast extract
1 teaspoon chopped chives
1 teaspoon chopped parsley

Peel, top and tail carrots, chop into small dice. Peel onions and slice thinly. Wash and slice mushrooms. Place carrots in large saucepan with a little water and cook 5 minutes. Drain. Add onions. Cover and cook over gentle heat 5 minutes, stirring often to prevent sticking or browning. Add mushrooms, cook 1 minute. Do not allow to brown. Remove hard stems from cabbage leaves and plunge them into boiling water for 4 minutes. Remove, rinse under cold water and pat dry. Line a greased 20cm spring-form tin with cabbage leaves, allow leaves to hang over edge of tin.

Combine eggs, milk powder and water with thyme, stir into onion mixture. Spoon filling evenly into prepared cake tin. Trim cabbage leaves to be level with top of filling. Grind all nuts in a blender and combine with remaining ingredients. Sprinkle topping over onion filling. Place cake tin in baking dish half-filled with cold water and bake at 200°C for 1 hour. Remove tin from water and allow to stand 5 minutes before opening spring tin. Slice and serve pie. N.B. Spinach leaves may be used instead of cabbage leaves.

Golden-topped vegetable casserole

1 eggplant
2 carrots
2 potatoes
2 onions
¼ cup olive oil
4 zucchini
4 tomatoes
2 cups okra, canned or fresh
¼ cup chopped parsley
2 teaspoons oregano
salt and pepper
¼ teaspoon nutmeg
3 cups mashed potato
½ cup grated cheese
2 eggs
½ cup milk

Slice eggplant, sprinkle with salt and allow to stand 30 minutes. Peel carrots, potatoes and slice. Plunge them into boiling water and simmer 5 minutes. Drain and rinse under cold water. Peel and slice onions. Rinse eggplant and pat dry. Fry onions in heated oil until soft. Remove and fry eggplant until golden brown. Slice zucchini and tomatoes. Top and tail okra. In a deep casserole layer all vegetables, sprinkling each layer with a little parsley, oregano, salt, pepper and nutmeg. Cover casserole and bake at 200°C for 30 minutes. Combine mashed potato, cheese, egg yolks, milk and paprika until smooth and creamy. Beat egg whites until stiff and fold into potato mixture. Spoon over casserole and place in oven. Bake at 190°C until top is golden.

Vegetable variations

Baked curried cabbage

½ cabbage
1 onion
2 whole cloves
1 bay leaf
½ teaspoon salt
1 cup basic light stock (recipe p.28)
1 tablespoon curry powder
1 tablespoon flour
2 tablespoons butter
¾ cup cream
1 cup soft breadcrumbs
2 tablespoons butter, extra

Pull cabbage apart and cut hard stems from each leaf. Shred cabbage finely. Peel onion and pierce it with cloves. Place onion, bay leaf, salt and stock in a saucepan and bring to the boil. Add cabbage and simmer 5 minutes. Drain cabbage, remove onion and bay leaf. Place cabbage in an oiled casserole. Combine curry, flour, butter and cream to make a smooth paste. Pour over cabbage. Sprinkle with breadcrumbs and butter and bake at 175°C for 15 minutes.

Baked leeks

6 leeks
1 clove garlic
1 cup soft brown breadcrumbs
salt and pepper
1 cup grated Cheddar cheese
1 tablespoon chopped chives

Cut root and green leafy top off leeks. Cut the white section into 1cm slices, place in colander and rinse thoroughly. Cook leeks in a small amount of boiling salted water for 10 minutes. Drain. Cut the garlic in half and rub over the inside of a shallow casserole dish. Discard garlic. Place one third of the leeks in the casserole, top with one third of the breadcrumbs, a little sprinkle of salt and pepper and one third of the cheese. Continue to layer until all ingredients are used. Sprinkle with chives and bake at 200°C for 15-20 minutes.

Leeks with pear and bean purée

8 leeks
300g green beans
2 pears
salt and pepper

Remove root and green top from leeks. Cut white in halves lengthwise. Wash thoroughly without allowing leeks to fall apart. Steam leeks until just tender, then keep warm over simmering water.

While leeks are cooking, make purée. Top, tail, and string beans. Peel, core, and quarter pears. Place these in saucepan of boiling water and boil 15 minutes. Drain and rinse in cold water. Purée in blender, adding a little water if necessary. Heat purée in bowl over boiling water. When warm place leeks on serving plate and pour purée over to serve.

Leeks with pear and bean purée

Mushrooms with zucchini sauce

2 zucchini
1 cup sour cream
1 tablespoon chopped chives
1 teaspoon chopped parsley
salt and pepper
2 egg yolks
500g small mushrooms
2 tablespoons butter

Wash zucchini and grate coarsely. Place on paper towel to remove moisture. Place sour cream, zucchini, chives, parsley, salt, pepper and lightly beaten egg yolks in saucepan and stir over gentle heat until mixture thickens. Keep warm but do not allow to boil. Slice mushrooms thinly and fry in butter until just tender. Drain and place on serving plate. Pour sauce over and serve immediately.

N.B. Zucchini sauce is also good with pan-fried potatoes, steamed broccoli, asparagus or steamed fennel.

Creamed beetroot

6 small beetroots
¼ cup vinegar

Sauce

1 tablespoon butter
1 tablespoon flour
1 cup milk
2 tablespoons cream
2 tablespoons horseradish cream
salt and pepper
chopped chives

Wash beetroot, cut off stalks 1cm above beetroot but do not remove root. Place in boiling water with vinegar and boil until tender, about 1 hour. When cooked, drain, cool slightly and rub skins off. Place beetroot in saucepan with a little butter and keep warm while making sauce. Melt butter, stir in flour and cook 1 minute. Add milk and cream and stir until sauce thickens and boils. Stir in horseradish, salt and pepper and simmer 2 minutes. Place beetroots on serving plate and cover with hot sauce. Serve immediately.

Soufflé potatoes

4 large old potatoes
1 cup grated Cheddar cheese
½ teaspoon salt
⅛ teaspoon pepper
4 tablespoons sour cream
1 tablespoon chopped chives
1 tablespoon chopped parsley
⅛ teaspoon paprika
2 egg yolks
3 egg whites

Wash potatoes, pierce with a skewer several times and bake at 180°C for 1½ hours. Potatoes should be soft but whole. Cut a lid off each potato and scoop out centre. Leave some potato on the skin to form a casing. Mash potato with all remaining ingredients except egg whites. Beat egg whites until stiff and gently fold into potato mixture. Spoon into potato cases. Place on an oven tray and bake at 200°C until tops are golden brown and puffy.

Soufflé potatoes

Mexican onions

6 medium onions
1 tablespoon butter
1 tablespoon plain flour
salt and chilli powder
⅓ cup milk
1 tablespoon chopped capsicum
¼ cup grated Cheddar cheese
¼ cup drained corn kernels

Place onions in boiling salt water and simmer for 10 minutes. Remove from water and cool slightly. Cut top and root from onion and peel carefully. Do not remove entire root or onion will fall apart. With a spoon remove centre from onions. Chop centres to make 2 tablespoons of chopped onions. Melt butter in saucepan, stir in flour, salt and chilli powder. Stir in milk until mixture thickens and boils. Add capsicum, cheese, corn and 2 tablespoons chopped onion. Spoon filling into onions allowing some to spill over sides. Place in a baking dish and bake at 200°C for 30 minutes.

Cheesy carrot ring

1kg young carrots
2 tablespoons butter
1 teaspoon salt
⅛ teaspoon pepper
1 cup light vegetable stock (recipe p.00)
125g button mushrooms
1 teaspoon olive oil
2 eggs
¼ cup grated Edam cheese
1 teaspoon chopped dill

Wash, peel and chop carrots finely. Heat butter in saucepan, add carrots and brown lightly. Add salt, pepper and stock, cover and simmer for 30 minutes. Wash and chop mushrooms. Fry in olive oil for 3 minutes. Drain. Place carrots in a bowl. Stir in lightly beaten eggs, cheese, dill and mushrooms. Grease a ring tin and line with greaseproof paper. Spoon mixture into tin and press down firmly. Cover with foil and place in a baking dish with 3cm water. Bake at 200°C for 20 minutes, reduce heat to 180°C and bake 20 minutes more. Allow to stand 10 minutes before turning out of tin onto serving plate.

Broad bean casserole

3 cups shelled broad beans
¼ teaspoon salt
1 tablespoon butter
1 bay leaf
1 cup tomato relish
⅛ teaspoon basil

Cook broad beans in small amount boiling water until just tender. Drain and place in a casserole with all other ingredients. Cover and bake at 180°C for 15 minutes. Remove cover and continue cooking another 15 minutes.

N.B. Frozen or drained canned beans may be used.

Tomato relish

4 under-ripe tomatoes
1 onion
1 stick celery
¼ cup horseradish cream
1 teaspoon salt
1 teaspoon prepared French mustard
2 tablespoons brown sugar
1 cup malt vinegar

Peel and chop tomatoes and onion. Chop celery. Place all ingredients in a saucepan, cover and simmer 45 minutes. Spoon into sterilised warm jars, seal and store in refrigerator.

Mexican onions

Spicy bean sprouts

500g fresh bean sprouts
2 tablespoons butter
1 teaspoon minced ginger
1 teaspoon minced garlic
2 onions
½ teaspoon turmeric
1 teaspoon cumin
½ teaspoon salt
¼ teaspoon paprika
1 teaspoon minced red chilli

Wash bean sprouts and drain well. Heat butter in frypan and cook ginger and garlic 1 minute. Peel and chop onions finely, cook 3 minutes. Add turmeric, cumin, salt, paprika and chilli and cook 3 minutes. Stir in sprouts, combine well and cook 3 minutes.

Broccoli in caper sauce

1 bunch broccoli
1 cup buttermilk
2 tablespoons cornflour
1 cup yoghurt
salt and pepper
2 teaspoons chopped capers
½ teaspoon turmeric
4 tablespoons sour cream

Trim broccoli stalks and slit from base to flower. Stand broccoli in boiling salted water and cook until stalks are just tender, about 8 minutes. Drain and cover to keep warm while preparing sauce. Blend buttermilk with cornflour and heat in saucepan, stirring occasionally. Add yoghurt, salt, pepper, capers and turmeric. Stir until mixture thickens. Add sour cream to thin down sauce. Place broccoli on serving plate, spoon some sauce over for garnish and serve remainder separately.

Fennel sauté

3 heads fennel
3 tablespoons butter
salt and pepper
grated rind ½ lemon
juice ½ lemon
1 tablespoon chopped parsley

Wash fennel and slice thinly. Melt butter in a pan, add fennel, cover and cook 5 minutes. Remove lid and cook further 5 minutes. Place on serving plate and keep warm. Add all remaining ingredients to pan and heat through then pour over warm fennel to serve.

Eggplant puff

1 x 500g eggplant
2 tablespoons butter
2 tablespoons flour
1 cup milk
4 eggs, separated
2 tablespoons chopped walnuts
⅛ teaspoon nutmeg
salt and pepper

Place eggplant in oven at 200°C for 30 minutes until pulp is soft. While eggplant is baking, melt butter in saucepan, stir in flour and cook 1 minute. Gradually add milk, stirring continuously until thickened and smooth. Stir egg yolks into sauce. Add walnuts, nutmeg, salt and pepper. Split eggplant, scrape out pulp, mash well and stir into sauce. Beat egg whites until stiff and fold into sauce. Pour mixture into oiled soufflé dish and bake at 190°C for 45 minutes. Serve immediately.

Broccoli in caper sauce

Eggplant puff

Springtime salad

3 cups cauliflorets
1 avocado
lemon juice
1 cup asparagus pieces
1 lettuce
¼ cup chopped shallots
2 tablespoons olive oil
4 tablespoons tarragon vinegar
1 teaspoon chopped parsley
salt and pepper
¼ teaspoon mustard
sesame seeds

Steam cauliflorets until tender but crisp. Refresh under cold water, pat dry. Halve avocado, remove seed and peel. Cube, sprinkle with lemon juice to prevent browning. Cover asparagus with boiling salt water, cook 5 minutes, refresh under cold water and pat dry. Wash and shred lettuce. Combine florets, avocado, asparagus, lettuce and shallots. Chill. Combine oil, vinegar, parsley, salt, pepper and mustard. Pour over salad, toss and serve garnished with toasted sesame seeds.

Poppy seed salad

1 lettuce
4 leaves spinach
1 cucumber
½ green capscium
½ cup chopped shallots

Dressing

¼ cup sugar
1 teaspoon salt
3 tablespoons lemon juice
4 tablespoons poppy seeds
2 teaspoons dry mustard
1 cup salad vinegar
¾ cup olive oil

Wash lettuce and spinach thoroughly and tear into bite-size pieces. Peel and cube cucumber. Shred capsicum into strips. Combine all vegetables in a salad bowl and refrigerate while preparing dressing. Mix sugar, mustard, salt, vinegar and lemon juice. Gradually beat in oil until dressing is thick. Use as much dressing as required for salad; leave the rest stored in a jar in the refrigerator.

Bean combo

½ cup cooked kidney beans
½ cup cooked soy beans
½ cup cooked lima beans
1 cup cooked green beans
1 tablespoon chopped parsley
1 cup shredded cabbage
½ cup chopped onion
2 tablespoons olive oil
4 tablespoons vinegar
salt and pepper

Combine all beans, parsley, cabbage and onion in a salad bowl. Mix oil, vinegar, salt, pepper and stir into salad. Chill well before serving.

Springtime salad

Macaroni and zucchini salad

250g zucchini
salt
1 cup sliced mushrooms
1 cup cooked wholemeal macaroni
¾ cup thin cream
¼ cup crunchy peanut butter
½ cup mayonnaise
1 tablespoon honey
1 tablespoon white vinegar
2 tablespoons lemon juice
½ cup roasted peanuts

Wash and slice zucchini. Place on kitchen paper, sprinkle with salt and allow to stand 30 minutes. Rinse under cold water and pat dry. Combine zucchini, mushrooms and macaroni in salad bowl. Chill while preparing dressing. Place all remaining ingredients except peanuts in blender and whip until smooth but not too thick. Coat salad lightly with dressing. Chill well and serve garnished with toasted peanuts. Extra dressing will keep well in refrigerator.

Tomatoes roquefort

4 tomatoes
1 onion
1 tablespoon chopped parsley
½ cup Roquefort cheese
2 tablespoons olive oil
2 tablespoons lemon juice
1 teaspoon sugar
salt, pepper, paprika

Wash tomatoes, slice thinly and place on serving platter. Peel onion, slice very thinly and place rings of onion over tomatoes. Blend all remaining ingredients until creamy and pour over. Chill before serving.

Apple salad

4 green apples
juice of 2 lemons
½ lettuce
1 cup cooked peas
½ cup chopped celery
¼ cup chopped walnuts
2 tablespoons olive oil
3 tablespoons vinegar
¼ teaspoon prepared mustard
salt and pepper

Peel, core and cube apples, and pour lemon juice over them to stop them from browning. Wash and shred lettuce then combine with apples, peas, celery and walnuts in salad bowl. Mix oil, vinegar, mustard, salt, pepper and pour over salad. Toss and serve.

Macaroni and zucchini salad

Farmhouse salad

350g cream cheese
1 cup grated Cheddar cheese
¼ cup cream
¼ cup chopped red capsicum
¼ cup chopped shallots
¼ cup pine nuts
3 teaspoons lemon juice
¼ teaspoon salt
¼ teaspoon paprika
1 lettuce
3 tomatoes
1 tablespoon chopped chives

Beat cream cheese until smooth. Beat in Cheddar cheese and cream until blended. Stir in capsicum, shallot, pine nuts, lemon juice, salt and paprika. Spread mixture into a freezer tray and chill until firm. Wash and shred lettuce. Wash and slice tomatoes. Place lettuce on a serving platter, top with tomatoes. Remove cheese from freezer and cut into cubes, place cubes on salad, sprinkle with chives and serve.

Fruit and nut salad

2 grapefruit, segmented
2 oranges, segmented
1 cup chopped pineapple
1 large green apple, cubed
1 tablespoon lemon juice
½ cup stuffed olives
½ lettuce
¼ cup toasted pine nuts
¼ cup toasted almonds
¼ cup chopped walnuts
1 tablespoon olive oil
2 tablespoons vinegar
salt and pepper
1 tablespoon chopped chives

Combine pineapple, grapefruit and orange segments, and chill. Toss apple in lemon juice to prevent browning and add. Top with olives. Wash and shred lettuce, place on serving platter. Spoon fruit mixture over lettuce and sprinkle with nuts. Combine oil, vinegar, salt, pepper, chives, and pour over salad just before serving.

Orange and spinach salad

½ bunch spinach, chopped
2 oranges
4 shallots, chopped
¼ cup toasted slivered almonds
2 tablespoons olive oil
1 tablespoon vinegar
1 tablespoon lemon juice
salt, pepper, pinch dry mustard

Wash spinach and remove stalks. Shred and drain in a colander. Peel and slice oranges. Combine spinach, shallots and almonds, place on serving platter. Place sliced oranges over spinach. Prepare dressing by combining oil, vinegar, lemon juice, salt, pepper and mustard. Cover with dressing and chill salad for 1 hour before serving.

Orange and spinach salad

Sicilian fennel salad

1 clove garlic
1 cucumber
1 onion
1 orange
4 tomatoes
1 bulb fennel
1 tablespoon oil
2 tablespoons lemon juice
salt and pepper
½ teaspoon chopped basil

Crush garlic and sprinkle over serving platter. Peel and slice cucumber, onion and orange into thin rounds. Wash and slice tomatoes. Wash and grate fennel. Layer salad vegetables on platter and chill. Combine oil, lemon juice, salt, pepper and basil in a jar, pour over salad and serve.

Russian red cabbage salad

6 cups shredded red cabbage
1 cinnamon stick
1 cup apple cider vinegar
1 green apple
extra lemon juice
1 cup sliced mushrooms
½ cup grated onion
1 tablespoon lemon juice
3 tablespoons yoghurt
salt and pepper
¼ teaspoon prepared mustard

Place cabbage in bowl with cinnamon stick. Heat vinegar, pour over cabbage, cover and allow to stand until cold. Drain all liquid and remove cinnamon stick. Peel, core and cut apple into cubes, sprinkle with lemon juice to prevent browning. Combine cabbage, apple, mushrooms and onion in salad bowl. Mix lemon juice, yoghurt, salt, pepper, mustard, and pour over salad to serve.

Potato nut salad

250g new potatoes
1 tablespoon olive oil
2 sticks celery
1 green apple
1 tablespoon lemon juice
¼ cup pine nuts
¼ cup chopped shallots
¼ cup chopped red capsicum
½ cup yoghurt
2 tablespoons tomato purée
salt and pepper
¼ teaspoon mustard powder

Boil potatoes in their jackets until tender. Cool, peel and chop into small cubes. Combine with oil. Wash and chop celery, add to potatoes. Remove core and chop apples into small cubes, toss in lemon juice to prevent browning, add to potatoes. Place potatoes, apple and celery in a salad bowl, stir in pine nuts, shallots and capsicum. Chill. Combine yoghurt, tomato purée, salt, pepper and mustard, pour over salad and serve garnished with toasted pine nuts.

Potato nut salad

Tropical rice salad

1 lettuce
2 cups cooked brown rice
1 cup chopped pineapple
¼ cup chopped celery
¼ cup chopped shallots
¼ cup chopped red capsicum
¼ cup corn kernels
¼ cup chopped walnuts
1 red apple
2 tablespoons lemon juice
1 tomato
1 tablespoon chopped parsley

Wash lettuce and line a salad bowl with best leaves. Shred remaining lettuce. Combine rice with pineapple, celery, shallots, capsicum, corn, walnuts and shredded lettuce. Add to bowl and chill. Core apple and chop into cubes, cover with lemon juice to prevent browning, add to salad. Cut tomato into wedges and place around edge of bowl. Sprinkle with parsley to serve.

Brown curried rice salad

3 cups cooked brown rice
½ cup diced red capsicum
½ cup tinned corn kernels
¼ cup chopped shallots
salt and pepper
¼ cup chopped celery
1 tablespoon salad oil
2 tablespoons tarragon vinegar
1 teaspoon chopped parsley
2 teaspoons curry powder

Combine rice, capsicum, corn, shallots, salt, pepper and celery in a salad bowl. Mix oil, vinegar, parsley and curry powder, pour over salad and toss.

For a party, increase quantities and place in separate bowls. Prepare dressing and coat rice, capsicum, corn and shallots lightly with dressing and toss. Layer in large glass salad bowl and chill before serving. Served like this it makes a spectacular party piece.

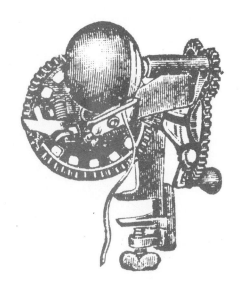

Brown curried rice salad

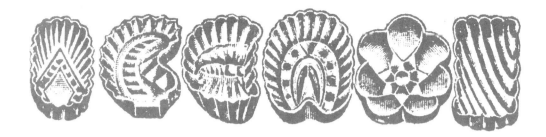

Orange surprise

1 cup fresh orange juice
1 packet orange jelly crystals
¾ cup boiling water
2 cups yoghurt
½ cup cream
orange or lemon butterflies

Cut oranges in halves, squeeze out juice and clean out pith so that orange skins can be used as serving dishes. Dissolve jelly in hot water and cool to room temperature. Stir in orange juice and then yoghurt until smooth. Refrigerate until mixture begins to set. Remove from refrigerator and whip until mixture is foamy. Beat cream until fluffy and fold into mixture. Spoon into halved orange cups and refrigerate until set. Serve garnished with orange or lemon butterflies or top with a little whipped cream.

Chinese pears

4 ripe pears
1 cinnamon stick
4 cloves
3 tablespoons chopped walnuts
3 tablespoons chopped dates
2 tablespoons honey
2 teaspoons ground ginger
slivered almonds

Peel pears, cut in half lengthwise and remove core. Place in baking dish, cut side up, with cinnamon and cloves. Combine walnuts, dates, honey and ginger to make a paste, fill pear cavities. Place pears in baking dish with a little water, cover with foil and bake at 180°C until pears are tender. Serve sprinkled with toasted slivered almonds.

Cream cheese pockets

3 tablespoons currants
4 tablespoons sweet sherry
2 glacé apricots
2 tablespoons chopped glacé ginger
3 tablespoons chopped hazelnuts
2 tablespoons sugar
2 cups Ricotta cheese
1 teaspoon mixed spice
8 sheets filo pastry
½ cup unsalted butter

Simmer currants in sherry for 10 minutes. Chop apricots and place in bowl with ginger, hazelnuts, sugar, cheese and mixed spice. Stir in currants. Cut filo pastry into halves across sheets. Brush each sheet with melted butter. Place 1 tablespoon of mixture on each sheet and fold up into a square parcel. Place squares on oiled baking tray and bake at 200°C for 10 minutes.

Rainbow rice pudding

½ cup chopped pitted prunes
½ cup chopped dried apricots
½ cup chopped raisins
1 cup boiling water
juice ½ lemon
2 cups cooked brown rice
½ teaspoon nutmeg
½ teaspoon cinnamon
2 egg yolks
1 cup milk

Soak fruit in water for 1 hour. Drain and stir in lemon juice. Combine rice with all remaining ingredients. Starting and finishing with a rice layer, put alternate layers of fruit and rice in a well greased soufflé dish. Cover dish and bake at 160°C for 1 hour. After removing from oven, stand dish in warm water for 10 minutes. Run knife around edge, then turn pudding out onto serving dish. May be served hot or cold.

Coconut cream custard

1 cup brown sugar
¼ cup water
2 cups coconut milk
4 eggs
½ teaspoon ground cardamom
¼ teaspoon nutmeg

Place sugar and water in saucepan and heat until sugar dissolves. Cool. Combine syrup with remaining ingredients and strain. Pour into individual cups and place in baking dish. Add a little cold water to baking dish and bake at 180°C for 1 hour or until custard is set. Cool, run knife around edge and turn out to serve.

N.B. To make coconut milk place 2 cups desiccated coconut in a blender with 2¼ cups hot water. Blend until smooth, strain through fine sieve and use liquid.

Pumpkin pie

Pastry

1 cup self-raising flour
1 cup wholemeal flour
½ cup butter
1 egg yolk
2 tablespoons lemon juice
iced water

Place flours in bowl and rub in butter. Combine egg yolk with lemon juice, work into dough. Add enough iced water to form a firm dough. Wrap in plastic and refrigerate 20 minutes. Roll out to fit 20cm pie plate and stand for 20 minutes in refrigerator.

Filling

350g cooked pumpkin
1 tablespoon brown sugar
2 eggs
4 tablespoons cream
¼ teaspoon nutmeg
¼ teaspoon ground ginger

Place pumpkin in blender with sugar, egg yolks, cream, nutmeg and ginger. Blend to a purée. Beat egg whites until stiff and fold into pumpkin. Pour mixture into pie plate and bake at 180°C for 35 minutes or until pastry is golden and filling has set. Serve warm.

Pumpkin pie

Poached peaches

4 peaches
¼ cup desiccated coconut
¼ cup ground almonds
½ teaspoon finely grated orange rind
1 egg yolk
2 tablespoons butter
1 cup white wine
1 cinnamon stick

Plunge peaches into boiling water and leave 1 minute. Drain, cover with cold water to cool. Peel, cut in half and remove stones. Place peaches, cut side up, in oven proof dish. Combine coconut, almonds, orange rind and egg yolk, spoon into peach cavities. Dot with butter. Pour in wine and add cinnamon stick. Cover and bake at 180°C for 20 minutes or until peaches are tender. Remove cinnamon stick and serve warm.

Ginger soufflé

3 tablespoons butter
3 tablespoons plain flour
1½ cups milk
2 tablespoons sugar
3 eggs
1 teaspoon vanilla essence
2 teaspoons grated ginger in syrup
icing sugar

Melt butter in saucepan, stir in flour and cook 1 minute. Add milk gradually to form a smooth sauce. Stir until sauce thickens and boils. Stir in sugar until dissolved. Cool sauce slightly. Separate eggs and beat yolks into sauce with vanilla essence and grated ginger. Beat egg whites until stiff and fold in sauce. Spoon mixture into soufflé dish and bake at 190°C for 40 minutes. Sprinkle with sieved icing sugar and serve immediately.

Apricot and nut flan

Pastry

1 cup plain flour
2 tablespoons chopped almonds
2 tablespoons chopped walnuts
1 tablespoon sugar
2 tablespoons butter
1 egg
2 tablespoons lemon juice
iced water

Place flour, nuts and sugar in a bowl and rub in butter. Combine egg and lemon juice, add to dough. Add enough cold water to form a firm dough. Wrap in plastic and allow to stand 20 minutes in refrigerator. Roll out to fit 18cm flan tin. Refrigerate while preparing filling.

Filling

1 x 425g can apricot halves
2 tablespoons chopped dried apricots
4 tablespoons chopped almonds
1 egg yolk
2 egg whites
4 tablespoons sugar
extra apricot halves for decoration if desired

Drain apricots and purée in blender or strain through a sieve. Mix in dried apricots, almonds and egg yolk. Beat egg whites until stiff, beat in sugar until dissolved. Fold into apricot mixture. Spoon mixture into flan and bake at 180°C for 1 hour. For a party decorate with additional apricot halves.

Apricot and nut flan

Pineapple calypso

1 ripe pineapple
6 tablespoons chopped fresh mint
2 egg whites
½ cup castor sugar

Peel pineapple and cut into quarters lengthwise. Remove hard core from centre of each quarter and cut pineapple into small cubes. Mix with mint and leave in refrigerator overnight.

Spoon pineapple into serving bowl. Beat egg whites until stiff, add half the sugar, beating until dissolved. Beat in remaining sugar until dissolved. Spoon meringue over pineapple and place under griller to brown.

Dried fruit crumble

1 cup dried apricots
1 cup dried figs
1 cup pitted prunes
¼ cup raisins
¼ cup currants
¼ cup sugar
1 cup water
¼ cup almonds
2 tablespoons flour
¼ cup desiccated coconut
¼ cup brown sugar
2 tablespoons butter

Soak fruit in enough water to cover for 1 hour. Drain. Place sugar and water in saucepan and bring to the boil. Add fruit and simmer for 30 minutes or until liquid has been absorbed. Add almonds and place mixture in ovenproof serving dish. Combine all remaining ingredients and sprinkle over fruit. Bake at 200°C until top is golden (15-20 minutes).

Strawberry sorbet

1 punnet strawberries
1 cup water
¼ cup sugar
½ cup ice cream
2 tablespoons lemon juice
2 tablespoons Kirsch
2 egg whites
¼ cup castor sugar

Wash and hull strawberries. Place strawberries, water, sugar, ice cream, lemon juice and Kirsch in a blender and purée. Pour mixture into 2 lamington tins and freeze. Beat egg whites until stiff. Add castor sugar and beat to dissolve. Remove strawberry ice from freezer and break up with a fork. Fold egg whites into strawberry mixture and spoon into individual serving bowls. Freeze, stirring every 10 minutes until mixture is firm.

Fruit brûlé

4 cups prepared fruit
1 cup cream
4 tablespoons brown sugar
¼ teaspoon cinnamon

Use any fruit in season for this dessert, such as grapes, peeled and seeded; cherries, seeded; apricots, quartered; strawberries, hulled; kiwi fruit, peeled and sliced. Place fruit into 4 individual serving dishes and pour ¼ cup cream into each. Leave in refrigerator overnight. Just before serving sprinkle 1 tablespoon brown sugar and a little cinnamon over each and place under griller until sugar melts and browns.

Strawberry sorbet

Orange and rhubarb compote

1 bunch rhubarb
2 oranges
½ cup brown sugar
¼ cup water

Wash rhubarb and trim stalks. Cut into 3cm lengths. Peel oranges, making sure all pith is removed. Cut into thin rounds and remove all pips. Layer fruit into baking dish and sprinkle with sugar. Add water, cover and bake at 185°C until rhubarb is tender. Serve hot or cold.

Apricot mousse

500g ripe apricots
juice ½ lemon
3 tablespoons icing sugar
2 teaspoons gelatine
½ cup cream
toasted slivered almonds

Plunge apricots into boiling water and leave 1 minute. Drain, cover with cold water to cool. Peel. Cut apricots in half and remove stones. Purée apricots with lemon juice and sugar in a blender or sieve. Place gelatine in ¼ cup cold water and stand over bowl of hot water until dissolved. Stir into apricot purée. Beat cream until stiff, fold into apricot mixture. Spoon into individual serving dishes and refrigerate until set. Serve garnished with toasted almond slivers.

N.B. Canned apricots may be used if well drained.

Caramel fruit dumplings

Caramel sauce

2 tablespoons butter
1 cup brown sugar
½ cup water
3 tablespoons Cointreau
1 tablespoon cornflour
½ cup cream

Place butter and sugar in saucepan and heat to melt butter. Combine all remaining ingredients and pour into saucepan. Stir over low heat until sugar dissolves, then bring to boil. Simmer for 3 minutes and keep warm.

Dumplings

1¼ cups self raising flour
¼ cup sugar
3 tablespoons butter
1 teaspoon vanilla essence
⅓ cup milk
¼ cup chopped dried apricots
¼ cup chopped dried apples
1 tablespoon currants

Place flour and sugar in bowl and rub in butter. Add vanilla, milk and knead in dried fruit. Dough should be quite soft. Form dough into 12 even sized balls. Drop 2 or 3 balls at a time into large pan of boiling water, cook rapidly for 10 minutes. Place on serving dish and coat with caramel sauce.

Caramel fruit dumplings

Apricot mousse and orange surprise

Weights and measures

Smaller measures are in standard cup measurements, or spoon measurements as set down by the Standards Association of Australia. These new metric measures have the stamp S2 on the jug set of cup measures and the set of measuring spoons. Always use level measures of the recommended utensils.

For easy conversion here are guidelines to assist you.

• DRY INGREDIENTS:		• LIQUIDS	
• Metric	• Avoirdupois	• Metric	• Imperial
15g	½oz.	30ml	1fl oz
30g	1oz	60ml (¼ cup)	2fl oz (¼ cup)
60g	2oz	100ml	3fl oz
90g	3oz	125ml (½ cup)	4fl oz (½ cup)
125g	4oz (¼lb)	150ml	5fl oz (¼pt)
155g	5oz	185ml (¾ cup)	6fl oz (¾ cup)
185g	6oz	250ml (1 cup)	8fl oz (1 cup)
220g	7oz	315ml (1¼ cups)	10fl oz (½pt)
250g	8oz (½lb)	375ml (1½ cups)	12fl oz (1½ cups)
280g	9oz	440ml (1¾ cups)	14fl oz (1¾ cups)
315g	10oz	500ml (2 cups)	16fl oz (2 cups)
345g	11oz	625ml (2½ cups)	20fl oz (1 pint)
375g	12oz (¾lb)		
410g	13oz		
440g	14oz		
470g	15oz		
500g (0.5kg)	16oz (1lb)		
750g (0.75kg)	24oz (1½lb)		
1000g (1kg)	32oz (2lb)		

- CUP MEASURES
  - 1 cup   =   250ml
  - ½ cup   =   125ml
  - ⅓ cup   =   83.3ml
  - ¼ cup   =   62.5ml

- SPOON MEASURES
  - 1 tablespoon (tblsp) =   20ml
  - 1 teaspoon (tsp)   =   5ml
  - ½ teaspoon (tsp)   =   2.5ml
  - ½ teaspoon (tsp)   =   1.25ml

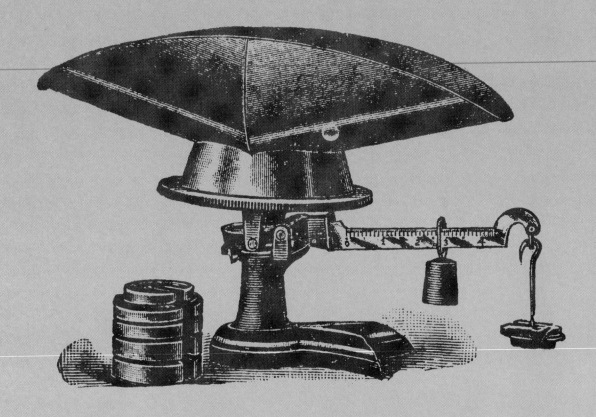

Tips for cooking beans

- Beans taste best when cooked in plenty of water. Reserve cooking water and use for cooking vegetables or add to soups.

- Always soak beans overnight if possible before cooking, it helps them to retain their shape and improves the texture.

- For extra flavour you can pan toast beans before cooking or soaking them.

- Add a little oil to the cooking water so they won't stick together in the pot.

- Always simmer beans covered with a lid. Add extra boiling water from time to time so that they don't dry out.

- Pressure cookers are ideal for beans — and you don't have to soak them first.

- Always cook more beans than needed: keep them handy for another meal. Store them in a covered container and place in the refrigerator.

Index

Breads
Anadama bread 11
Banana bran muffins 15
Basic wholemeal bread 9
Cheese popovers 15
Corn meal muffins 12
Cottage oatmeal loaf 14
Fruit and nut twists 15
Gingerbread 12
Mixed grain loaf 11
Pumpernickel 10
Rye and soy loaf 11
Seed buns 14

Tasty nibbles
Carrot and walnut tidbits 24
Cheese puffs 22
Empanadas 20
Hot cheese balls 20
Piquant apricots 20
Potato sticks 24
Rice croquettes with tomato dip 19
Spiced tomato appetisers 24
Vegetable pâté 19
Wholemeal salad tartlets 22

Unusual hot soups
Almond and grape soup 28
Basic dark vegetable stock 28
Basic light vegetable stock 28
Buttermilk soup 30
Cream of choko soup 30
Cream of watercress soup 30
Farmhouse chowder 34
Pea and barley soup 34
Plum soup 32
Two bean soup 32

Appetite stirrers
Asparagus timbales 36

Black-eyed Susans 44
Crunchy nut terrine 38
Mushroom casserole 40
Mushroom custards 42
Pears in tarragon 42
Roquefort mousse 44
Soyaroni casserole 44
Spinach rolls 38
Stuffed turnips 36
Tomato granita 40
Vegeroni Alfredo 42
Vegetable tacos 40

Main Events
Baked vegetable ring 52
Bean-filled marrow 54
Crispy cheese flan 57
Crunchy onion pie 58
Cuban eggs 50
Flan indienne 56
Golden-topped vegetable casserole 58
Hot rice salad 56
Individual moussakas 47
Instant bean medley 56
Okra casserole 47
Ribbon bean bake 52
Rice pie 54
Spinach roulade 50

Vegetable variations
Baked curried cabbage 60
Baked leeks 60
Broad bean casserole 64
Broccoli in caper sauce 66
Cheesy carrot ring 64
Creamed beetroot 62
Eggplant puff 66
Fennel sauté 66

Leeks with pear and bean purée 60
Mexican onions 64
Mushroom with zucchini sauce 62
Soufflé potatoes 62
Spicy bean sprouts 66

Cool salads
Apple salad 72
Bean combo 71
Brown curried rice salad 78
Farmhouse salad 74
Fruit and nut salad 74
Macaroni and zucchini salad 72
Orange and spinach salad 74
Poppy seed salad 71
Potato nut salad 76
Russian red cabbage salad 76
Sicilian fennel salad 76
Springtime salad 71
Tomatoes roquefort 72
Tropical rice salad 78

Desserts for a sweet tooth
Apricot and nut flan 84
Apricot mousse 88
Caramel fruit dumplings 88
Chinese pears 81
Coconut cream custard 82
Cream cheese pockets 81
Dried fruit crumble 86
Fruit brûlé 86
Ginger soufflé 84
Orange and rhubarb compote 88
Orange surprise 81
Pineapple calypso 86
Poached peaches 84
Pumpkin pie 82
Rainbow rice pudding 82
Strawberry sorbet 86